Plastic Bottles and Bags

Kate Walker

Marshall Cavendish
Benchmark
New York

Other Marshall Cavendish Offices:
Marshall Cavendish International (Asia) Private Limited, 1 New Industrial Road, Singapore 536196 • Marshall Cavendish International (Thailand) Co Ltd. 253 Asoke, 12th Flr, Sukhumvit 21 Road, Klongtoey Nua, Wattana, Bangkok 10110, Thailand • Marshall Cavendish (Malaysia) Sdn Bhd, Times Subang, Lot 46, Subang Hi-Tech Industrial Park, Batu Tiga, 40000 Shah Alam, Selangor Darul Ehsan, Malaysia

Marshall Cavendish is a trademark of Times Publishing Limited

All websites were available and accurate when this book was sent to press.

Library of Congress Cataloging-in-Publication Data

Walker, Kate.
     Plastic bottles and bags / Kate Walker.
        p. cm. — (Recycling)
     Includes index.
     Summary: "Discusses how plastic bottles and bags are made and the variety
     of ways to recycle them"—Provided by publisher.
     ISBN 978-1-60870-133-9
     1. Plastic bottles—Recycling—Juvenile literature. 2. Plastic
     bags—Recycling—Juvenile literature. I. Title.
     TD798.W35 2011
     668.4'192—dc22
                              2009041326

First published in 2009 by
MACMILLAN EDUCATION AUSTRALIAN PTY LTD
15–19 Claremont Street, South Yarra 3141

Visit our website at www.macmillan.com.au or go directly to www.macmillanlibrary.com.au

Associated companies and representatives throughout the world.

Copyright © Kate Walker 2009

Edited by Julia Carlomagno
Text and cover design by Christine Deering
Page layout by Christine Deering
Photo research by Legend Images
Illustrations by Gaston Vanzet

Printed in the United States

Acknowledgments
The author and the publisher are grateful to the following for permission to reproduce copyright material:

Front cover photograph: Father and son recycling plastic bottles, photo by Dev Carr/Getty Images

Photos courtesy of: Coo-ee Picture Library, **15**, **22**; © Creatas, **30** top; The DW Stock Picture Library, **7**; © David Granville/Fotolia.com, **30** bottom; Dev Carr/Getty Images, **1**; Peter Ginter/Getty Images, **3**, **13** right; Mark Segal/Getty Images, **16**; Kevin Spreekmeester/Getty Images, **17**; Kim Steele/ Getty Images, **9** bottom; © Monika Adamczyk/iStockphoto, **6**; © Sorin Alb/iStockphoto, **12** left; © Peter Bokhorst/iStockphoto, **30** center; © Ralph125/ iStockphoto, **5**; © 2008 Jupiterimages, **14**; Kilby Shores Elementary School, **28**, **29**; © Peter E. Smith, Natural Sciences Image Library, **13** left, **18**; Photolibrary, **9** center; Photolibrary/Colin Monteath, **12** center; Photolibrary/James King-Holmes/SPL, **12** right; © Galyna Andrushko/Shutterstock, **21**; © Stephen Coburn/Shutterstock, **8**; © Christopher Jones/Shutterstock, **4**; © Lorraine Kourafas/Shutterstock, **23**; © Robert Kyllo/Shutterstock, **20**; © V. J. Matthew/Shutterstock, **9** left; Stratherrick Primary School, **26**, **27**.

While every care has been taken to trace and acknowledge copyright, the publisher tenders their apologies for any accidental infringement where copyright has proved untraceable. Where the attempt has been unsuccessful, the publisher welcomes information that would redress the situation.

Contents

Glossary Words

When a word is printed in **bold**, you can look up its meaning in the Glossary on page 31.

What Is Recycling?

Recycling is collecting used products and making them into new products. Recycling is easy and keeps the environment clean.

Every plastic bottle that is recycled saves resources and helps the environment.

Why Recycle Plastic Bottles and Bags?

Recycling plastic bottles and bags helps:

- save **natural resources** for future use
- reduce **pollution** in the environment
- keep waste material out of **landfills**

If more plastic bottles and bags were recycled, landfills such as this one could be closed.

Plastic Bottles and Bags

People use plastic bottles and bags every day.
Plastic bottles are used for:

- drinks
- milk
- shampoo
- cleaning products

Plastic bottles are used as containers for drinks.

Plastic bags are used for:

- shopping bags
- food packaging
- product packaging
- lunch bags
- garbage-can liners

Plastic bags are often used for carrying groceries home from the supermarket.

How Plastic Is Made

Plastic is made from **crude oil**. Crude oil is a valuable natural resource that may be used up by the year 2050.

Oil wells draw crude oil out of the ground to make plastic.

The Plastic-Making Process

Crude oil goes through a three-stage **process** called **distilling** to make plastic.

Stage 1
Crude oil is heated in a tower and separated into solids, liquids, and gases.

Stage 2
Gases are taken out of the tower.

Stage 3
Gases are mixed with chemicals that turn them into solid plastics.

Throwing Away Plastic or Recycling Plastic?

Throwing away plastic uses natural resources, increases pollution, and adds to waste.

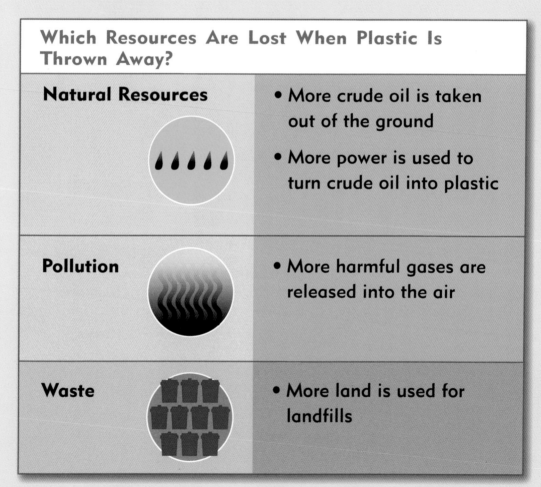

Which Resources Are Lost When Plastic Is Thrown Away?

Natural Resources	• More crude oil is taken out of the ground • More power is used to turn crude oil into plastic
Pollution	• More harmful gases are released into the air
Waste	• More land is used for landfills

Recycling plastic saves natural resources, reduces pollution, and cuts down on waste. Which do you think is better, wasting or recycling plastic?

Which Resources Are Saved When Plastic Is Recycled?

Natural resources	• Less crude oil is taken out of the ground • Less power is used to turn crude oil into plastic
Pollution	• Fewer harmful gases escape into the air
Waste	• Less land is used for landfills

How Plastic Is Recycled

Plastic is recycled through a five-stage process. This process begins when we recycle used plastic bottles or bags. It ends with new plastic products.

Stage 1

Used plastic bottles are collected from curbside recycling bins. Plastic bags are collected from supermarket plastic-bag recycling bins.

Stage 2

Different types of plastic are separated into **pure streams**.

Stage 3

Plastic is shredded into flakes. The plastic flakes are washed to remove labels, oil, and food.

Stage 4

Plastic flakes are
heated in a machine
until they melt.

Stage 5

Melted plastic is
made into new
plastic products.

Recycling Plastic at Home

Most households have special recycling bins.
All **recyclable** plastic can be put into these bins.

Plastic is put into recycling bins so it can be collected
by recycling trucks.

How to Recycle Plastic

The correct way to recycle plastic bottles is:
- rinse bottles clean with water
- remove bottle lids
- squash bottles flat

Rinse bottles with water to make sure they are clean before recycling them.

Recycling Plastic at School

School cafeterias often sell drinks in plastic bottles. Most lunchrooms have a special plastic-recycling bin. A team of **monitors** looks after the bin.

A plastic-recycling bin in a lunch area reminds students to recycle their plastic.

Plastic-Recycling Monitors

Plastic-recycling monitors:

- take turns to empty the recycling bin
- hand out awards to students who recycle plastic
- check that no other trash has gone into the bin

Monitors in some schools hand out awards to students who regularly recycle plastic.

Can All Plastic Be Recycled?

Not all plastic can be recycled. In most areas only Code 1 and Code 2 plastic containers can be recycled.

Most plastic products have their code number stamped on the bottom.

Code 1 and Code 2 plastic bottles are recycled to make new products. **Nonrecyclable** plastic products should go in the garbage can.

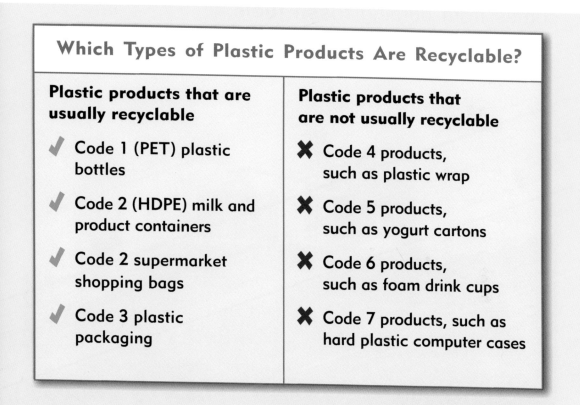

Which Types of Plastic Products Are Recyclable?

Plastic products that are usually recyclable	Plastic products that are not usually recyclable
✓ Code 1 (PET) plastic bottles	✗ Code 4 products, such as plastic wrap
✓ Code 2 (HDPE) milk and product containers	✗ Code 5 products, such as yogurt cartons
✓ Code 2 supermarket shopping bags	✗ Code 6 products, such as foam drink cups
✓ Code 3 plastic packaging	✗ Code 7 products, such as hard plastic computer cases

Is Recycling Plastic the Best Option?

Recycling plastic saves crude oil and helps the environment. However, recycling plastic also uses resources. Heat used to clean and reshape plastic comes from burning **fossil fuels**.

Coal is a fossil fuel that generates heat to recycle plastic.

Used plastic has to be cleaned with **caustic soda** and water before it is recycled. Caustic soda is a harsh chemical that can pollute waterways.

Recycling plastic can cause pollution in natural waterways such as this one.

Reducing and Reusing Plastic

There are many ways to reduce plastic use or to reuse plastic products. One way is to take your own bag when you go shopping.

A simple way to reduce plastic use is to use a cloth bag to carry groceries.

Some simple ways to reuse plastic are:
- refill used plastic bottles
- pack food in reusable plastic containers
- line garbage cans with used paper bags or newspaper instead of plastic bags.

Pack school lunches in reusable plastic containers.

Make a Plastic Space Capsule and Parachute

Plastic bottles and bags are very lightweight. Build a space capsule using a yogurt tub and a plastic bag.

What You Will Need:

- one used plastic bag
- one yogurt tub (32 oz) with a snap-on lid
- scissors
- four pieces of string about 8 inches (20 cm) long

What to Do:

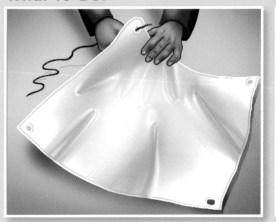

1. Cut a 16 inch x 16 inch (40 cm x 40 cm) square from the plastic bag and make a hole in each corner. Tie a piece of string through each hole.

2. Make two pairs of string by knotting each pair together 3 inches (8 cm) from the plastic. Place the strings inside the plastic tub with the knots just beneath the rim.

3. Press on the lid of the tub. One pair of strings should be on each side. Fold the plastic parachute in half and hold it against the lid.

4. Toss the plastic tub into the air. The parachute will open as the tub falls to the ground.

School Recycling Projects

Students at Stratherrick Primary School in Scotland grow vegetables all year round. Plants are protected from cold weather inside hothouses made of used plastic bottles.

Students made hothouses by wiring plastic bottles together inside a wooden frame.

The plastic bottles trap and hold warmth from the Sun, even on cold winter days. The hothouses also trap moisture, which means plants need less watering.

Stratherrick Primary School students grow many sorts of vegetables in their plastic-bottle hothouses.

Recycling Plastic Bags

Students of Kilby Shores Elementary School, in Virginia, are proud recyclers. In 2009 they collected 63,085 plastic bags for recycling in just three months.

Students counted and bundled the used plastic bags.

The bags were sent to Trex, a company that makes outdoor building materials. Trex mixes waste wood and melted plastic bags to make material for things such as decks and fences.

Students at Kilby Shores Elementary School were given a bench made from Trex recycled material.

How Recycling Plastic helps Animals

Plastic creates litter. Some animals are harmed when they eat litter. When you recycle plastic you reduce litter and save the lives of animals, including:

- seals

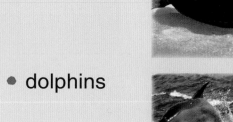

- dolphins

- whales

Glossary

caustic soda   A harsh cleaning chemical.

crude oil   A dark, oily substance taken from the ground to make plastic and other products.

distilling   A process that separates crude oil into solids, liquids, and gases.

fossil fuels   Oil-based fuels that power engines in cars and trucks.

landfills   Large holes in the ground where garbage is buried.

monitors   Students who are given special duties.

natural resources   Materials found in nature that people use and value.

nonrecyclable   Not able to be recycled.

pollution   Waste that damages the air, water, or land.

process   A series of actions that brings about a change.

pure streams   Groups of items made of the same material.

recyclable   Able to be recycled.

Index